EDINBURGH

"A Royal Proclamation

EDINBURGH

Picturesque Notes

by

Robert Louis Stevenson

BARNES
&NOBLE
BOOKS
NEW YORK

This edition published by Barnes & Noble, Inc.

1993 Barnes & Noble Books

ISBN 1-56619-278-1

Printed and bound in the United States of America

M 9 8 7 6 5 4 3 2 1

EDINBURGH

CHAPTER I.

Introductory.

THE ancient and famous metropolis of the
North sits overlooking a windy estuary
from the slope and summit of three hills. No
situation could be more commanding for the head
city of a kingdom ; none better chosen for noble
prospects. From her tall precipice and terraced
gardens she looks far and wide on the sea and
broad champaigns. To the east you may catch
at sunset the spark of the May lighthouse, where
the Firth expands into the German Ocean ; and
away to the west, over all the carse of Stirling,
you can see the first snows upon Ben Ledi.

But Edinburgh pays cruelly for her high seat
in one of the vilest climates under heaven. She
is liable to be beaten upon by all the winds that

blow, to be drenched with rain, to be buried in
cold sea fogs out of the east, and powdered with
the snow as it comes flying southward from the
Highland hills. The weather is raw and boister-
ous in winter, shifty and ungenial in summer,
and a downright meteorological purgatory in the
spring. The delicate die early, and I, as a sur-
vivor, among bleak winds and plumping rain,
have been sometimes tempted to envy them their
fate. For all who love shelter and the blessings
of the sun, who hate dark weather and perpetual
tilting against squalls, there could scarcely be
found a more unhomely and harassing place
of residence. Many such aspire angrily after
that Somewhere-else of the imagination, where all
troubles are supposed to end. They lean over
the great bridge which joins the New Town with
the Old — that windiest spot, or high altar, in
this northern temple of the winds — and watch
the trains smoking out from under them and
vanishing into the tunnel on a voyage to brighter
skies. Happy the passengers who shake off the
dust of Edinburgh, and have heard for the last
time the cry of the east wind among her chimney-
tops! And yet the place establishes an interest

in people's hearts; go where they will, they find no city of the same distinction; go where they will, they take a pride in their old home.

Venice, it has been said, differs from all other cities in the sentiment which she inspires. The rest may have admirers; she only, a famous fair one, counts lovers in her train. And, indeed, even by her kindest friends, Edinburgh is not considered in a similar sense. These like her for many reasons, not any one of which is satisfactory in itself. They like her whimsically, if you will, and somewhat as a virtuoso dotes upon his cabinet. Her attraction is romantic in the narrowest meaning of the term. Beautiful as she is, she is not so much beautiful as interesting. She is pre-eminently Gothic, and all the more so since she has set herself off with some Greek airs, and erected classic temples on her crags. In a word, and above all, she is a curiosity. The Palace of Holyrood has been left aside in the growth of Edinburgh, and stands grey and silent in a workman's quarter and among breweries and gas works. It is a house of many memories. Great people of yore, kings and queens, buffoons and grave ambassadors, played their stately farce for centuries in Holyrood. Wars have been plotted, dancing has lasted deep into the night, murder has been done in its chambers. There Prince Charlie held his phantom levées, and in a

Gate of Holyrooa.

very gallant manner represented a fallen dynasty for some hours. Now, all these things of clay are mingled with the dust, the king's crown itself is shown for sixpence to the vulgar; but the stone palace has outlived these charges. For fifty weeks together, it is no more than a show for tourists and a museum of old furniture; but on the fifty-first, behold the palace reawakened and mimicking its past. The Lord Commissioner, a kind of stage sovereign, sits among stage courtiers; a coach and six and clattering escort come and go before the gate; at night, the windows are lighted up, and its near neighbours, the workmen, may dance in their own houses to the palace music. And in this the palace is typical. There is a spark among the embers; from time to time the old volcano smokes. Edinburgh has but partly abdicated, and still wears, in parody, her metropolitan trappings. Half a capital and half a country town, the whole city leads a double existence; it has long trances of the one and flashes of the other; like the king of the Black Isles, it is half alive and half a monumental marble. There are armed men and cannon in the citadel overhead; you may see the troops marshalled on the high parade; and at night after the early winter evenfall, and in the morning before the laggard winter dawn, the wind carries abroad over Edinburgh

the sound of drums and bugles. Grave judges sit
bewigged in what was once the scene of imperial
deliberations. Close by in the High Street perhaps the trumpets may sound about the stroke
of noon ; and you see a troop of citizens in
tawdry masquerade ; tabard above, heather-mix-
ture trowser below, and the men themselves
trudging in the mud among unsympathetic by-
standers. The grooms of a well-appointed circus
tread the streets with a better presence. And
yet these are the Heralds and Pursuivants of
Scotland, who are about to proclaim a new law
of the United Kingdom before two-score boys,
and thieves, and hackney-coachmen. Meanwhile
every hour the bell of the University rings out
over the hum of the streets, and every hour a
double tide of students, coming and going, fills
the deep archways. And lastly, one night in the
springtime—or say one morning rather, at the
peep of day—late folk may hear voices of many
men singing a psalm in unison from a church
on one side of the old High Street ; and a little
after, or perhaps a little before, the sound of
many men singing a psalm in unison from another
church on the opposite side of the way. There

will be something in the words above the dew
of Hermon, and how goodly it is to see brethren
dwelling together in unity. And the late folk
will tell themselves that all this singing denotes
the conclusion of two yearly ecclesiastical parliaments—the parliaments of Churches which are
brothers in many admirable virtues, but not
specially like brothers in this particular of a
tolerant and peaceful life.

Again, meditative people will find a charm in
a certain consonancy between the aspect of the
city and its odd and stirring history. Few
places, if any, offer a more barbaric display of
contrasts to the eye. In the very midst stands
one of the most satisfactory crags in nature—a
Bass Rock upon dry land, rooted in a garden
shaken by passing trains, carrying a crown of
battlements and turrets, and describing its war-
like shadow over the liveliest and brightest
thoroughfare of the new town. From their
smoky beehives, ten stories high, the unwashed
look down upon the open squares and gardens
of the wealthy ; and gay people sunning themselves along Princes Street, with its mile of com-
mercial palaces all beflagged upon some great

occasion, see, across a gardened valley set with statues, where the washings of the Old Town flutter in the breeze at its high windows. And then, upon all sides, what a clashing of architecture ! In this one valley, where the life of the town goes most busily forward, there may be seen, shown one above and behind another by the accidents of the ground, buildings in almost every style upon the globe. Egyptian and Greek temples, Venetian palaces and Gothic spires, are huddled one over another in a most admired disorder ; while, above all, the brute mass of the Castle and the summit of Arthur's Seat look down upon these imitations with a becoming dignity, as the works of Nature may look down the monuments of Art. But Nature is a more indiscriminate patroness than we imagine, and in no way frightened of a strong effect. The birds roost as willingly among the Corinthian capitals as in the crannies of the crag ; the same atmosphere and daylight clothe the eternal rock and yesterday's imitation portico ; and as the soft northern sunshine throws out everything into a glorified distinctness — or easterly mists, coming up with the blue evening, fuse

all these incongruous features into one, and the
lamps begin to glitter along the street, and faint
lights to burn in the high windows across the
valley—the feeling grows upon you that this
also is a piece of nature in the most intimate
sense ; that this profusion of eccentricities, this
dream in masonry and living rock, is not a
drop-scene in a theatre, but a city in the world
of every-day reality, connected by railway and
telegraph-wire with all the capitals of Europe,
and inhabited by citizens of the familiar type,
who keep ledgers, and attend church, and have
sold their immortal portion to a daily paper. By
all the canons of romance, the place demands
to be half deserted and leaning towards decay ;
birds we might admit in profusion, the play of
the sun and winds, and a few gipsies encamped
in the chief thoroughfare ; but these citizens,
with their cabs and tramways, their trains and
posters, are altogether out of key. Chartered
tourists, they make free with historic localities,
and rear their young among the most picturesque
sites with a grand human indifference. To see
them thronging by, in their neat clothes and
conscious moral rectitude, and with a little air

of possession that verges on the absurd, is not the least striking feature of the place.*

And the story of the town is as eccentric as its appearance. For centuries it was a capital thatched with heather, and more than once, in the evil days of English invasion, it has gone up in flame to heaven, a beacon to ships at sea. It was the jousting-ground of jealous nobles, not only on Greenside, or by the King's Stables, where set tournaments were fought to the sound of trumpets and under the authority of the royal presence, but in every alley where there was room to cross swords, and in the main street,

---

* These sentences have, I hear, given offence in my native town, and a proportionable pleasure to our rivals of Glasgow. I confess the news caused me both pain and merriment. May I remark, as a balm for wounded fellow-townsmen, that there is nothing deadly in my accusations? Small blame to them if they keep ledgers: 'tis an excellent business habit. Churchgoing is not, that ever I heard, a subject of reproach; decency of linen is a mark of prosperous affairs, and conscious moral rectitude one of the tokens of good living. It is not their fault if the city calls for something more specious by way of inhabitants. A man in a frock-coat looks out of place upon an Alp or Pyramid, although he has the virtues of a Peabody and the talents of a Bentham. And let them console themselves—they do as well as anybody else; the population of (let us say) Chicago would cut quite as rueful a figure on the same romantic stage. To the Glasgow people I would say only one word, but that is of gold: *I have not yet written a book about Glasgow.*

where popular tumult under the Blue Blanket alternated with the brawls of outlandish clans-men and retainers. Down in the palace John Knox reproved his queen in the accents of modern democracy. In the town, in one of those little shops plastered like so many swallows' nests among the buttresses of the old Cathedral, that familiar autocrat, James VI., would gladly share a bottle of wine with George Heriot the goldsmith. Up on the Pentland Hills, that so quietly look down on the Castle with the city lying in waves around it, those mad and dismal fanatics, the Sweet Singers, haggard from long exposure on the moors, sat day and night with 'tearful psalmns' to see Edinburgh consumed with fire from heaven, like another Sodom or Gomorrah. There, in the Grass-market, stiff-necked, covenanting heroes, offered up the often unnecessary, but not less honourable, sacrifice of their lives, and bade eloquent farewell to sun, moon, and stars, and earthly friendships, or died silent to the roll of drums. Down by yon outlet rode Grahame of Claverhouse and his thirty dragoons, with the town beating to arms behind their horses' tails—a sorry handful thus riding

for their lives, but with a man at the head who
was to return in a different temper, make a dash
that staggered Scotland to the heart, and die
happily in the thick of fight.   There Aikenhead
was hanged for a piece of boyish incredulity ;
there, a few years afterwards, David Hume
ruined Philosophy and Faith, an undisturbed and
well-reputed citizen ; and thither, in yet a few
years more, Burns came from the plough-tail,
as to an academy of gilt unbelief and artificial
letters.   There, when the great exodus was made
across the valley, and the New Town began to
spread abroad its draughty parallelograms, and
rear its long frontage on the opposing hill, there
was such a flitting, such a change of domicile
and dweller, as was never excelled in the history
of cities : the cobbler succeeded the earl ; the
beggar ensconced himself by the judge's chimney ;
what had been a palace was used as a pauper
refuge ; and great mansions were so parcelled
out among the least and lowest in society, that
the hearthstone of the old proprietor was thought
large enough to be partitioned off into a bedroom
by the new.

CHAPTER II.

Old Town — The Lands.

THE Old Town, it is pretended, is the chief characteristic, and, from a picturesque point of view, the liver-wing of Edinburgh. It is one of the most common forms of depreciation to throw cold water on the whole by adroit over-commendation of a part, since everything worth judging, whether it be a man, a work of art, or only a fine city, must be judged upon its merits as a whole. The Old Town depends for much of its effect on the new quarters that lie around it, on the sufficiency of its situation, and on the hills that back it up. If you were to set it some-where else by itself, it would look remarkably like Stirling in a bolder and loftier edition. The point is to see this embellished Stirling planted in the midst of a large, active, and fantastic modern city; for there the two re-act in a pic-turesque sense, and the one is the making of the other.

The Old Town occupies a sloping ridge or tail of diluvial matter, protected, in some subsidence of the waters, by the Castle cliffs which fortify it to the west. On the one side of it and the other the new towns of the south and of the north occupy their lower, broader, and more gentle hill-tops. Thus, the quarter of the Castle overtops the whole city and keeps an open view to sea and land. It dominates for miles on every side; and people on the decks of ships, or ploughing in quiet country places over in Fife, can see the banner on the Castle battlements, and the smoke of the Old Town blowing abroad over the subjacent country. A city that is set upon a hill. It was, I suppose, from this distant aspect that she got her nickname of *Auld Reekie.* Perhaps it was given her by people who had never crossed her doors : day after day, from their various rustic Pisgahs, they had seen the pile of building on the hill-top, and the long plume of smoke over the plain ; so it appeared to them ; so it had appeared to their fathers tilling the same field ; and as that was all they knew of the place, it could be all expressed in these two words.

Indeed, even on a nearer view, the Old Town

Cowfeeder Row and Head of West Port.

is properly smoked ; and though it is well washed
with rain all the year round, it has a grim and
sooty aspect among its younger suburbs.   It
grew, under the law that regulates the growth
of walled cities in precarious situations, not in
extent, but in height and density.   Public buildings were forced, wherever there was room for
them, into the midst of thoroughfares ; thoroughfares were diminished into lanes ; houses sprang
up story after story, neighbour mounting upon
neighbour's shoulder, as in some Black Hole of
Calcutta, until the population slept fourteen or
fifteen deep in a vertical direction.   The tallest
of these *lands*, as they are locally termed, have
long since been burnt out ; but to this day it is
not uncommon to see eight or ten windows at a
flight ; and the cliff of building which hangs
imminent over Waverley Bridge would still put
many natural precipices to shame.   The cellars
are already high above the gazer's head, planted
on the steep hill-side ; as for the garret, all the
furniture may be in the pawn-shop, but it commands a famous prospect to the Highland hills.
The poor man may roost up there in the centre
of Edinburgh, and yet have a peep of the green

country from his window ; he shall see the quarters
of the well-to-do fathoms underneath, with their
broad squares and gardens ; he shall have nothing
overhead but a few spires, the stone top-gallants
of the city ; and perhaps the wind may reach
him with a rustic pureness, and bring a smack
of the sea, or of flowering lilacs in the spring.

It is almost the correct literary sentiment to
deplore the revolutionary improvements of Mr.
Chambers and his following. It is easy to be a
conservator of the discomforts of others ; indeed,
it is only our good qualities we find it irksome
to conserve. Assuredly, in driving streets through
the black labyrinth, a few curious old corners
have been swept away, and some associations
turned out of house and home. But what slices
of sunlight, what breaths of clean air, have been
let in ! And what a picturesque world remains
untouched ! You go under dark arches, and down
dark stairs and alleys. The way is so narrow
that you can lay a hand on either wall ; so steep
that, in greasy winter weather, the pavement is
almost as treacherous as ice. Washing dangles
above washing from the windows ; the houses
bulge outwards upon flimsy brackets ; you see a

bit of sculpture in a dark corner ; at the top of all, a gable and a few crowsteps are printed on the sky.   Here, you come into a court where the children are at play and the grown people sit upon their doorsteps, and perhaps a church spire shows itself above the roofs.   Here, in the narrowest of the entry, you find a great old mansion still erect, with some insignia of its former state— some scutcheon, some holy or courageous motto, on the lintel.   The local antiquary points out where famous and well-born people had their lodging ; and as you look up, out pops the head of a slatternly woman from the countess's window. The Bedouins camp within Pharaoh's palace walls, and the old war-ship is given over to the rats. We are already a far way from the days when powdered heads were plentiful in these alleys, with jolly, port-wine faces underneath.   Even in the chief thoroughfares Irish washings flutter at the windows, and the pavements are encumbered with loiterers.

These loiterers are a true character of the scene.   Some shrewd Scotch workmen may have paused on their way to a job, debating Church affairs and politics with their tools upon their

Old Bow-Head, Lawnmarket, Edinburgh.

arm.   But the most part are of a different order
—skulking jail-birds ; unkempt, bare-foot children ; big-mouthed, robust women, in a sort of
uniform of striped flannel petticoat and short
tartan shawl ; among these, a few surpervising
constables and a dismal sprinkling of mutineers
and broken men from higher ranks in society,
with some mark of better days upon them, like
a brand.   In a place no larger than Edinburgh,
and where the traffic is mostly centred in five
or six chief streets, the same face comes often
under the notice of an idle stroller.   In fact, from
this point of view, Edinburgh is not so much a
small city as the largest of small towns.   It is
scarce possible to avoid observing your neighbours ; and I never yet heard of any one who
tried.   It has been my fortune, in this anony-
mous accidental way, to watch more than one
of these downward travellers for some stages on
the road to ruin.   One man must have been upwards of sixty before I first observed him, and
he made then a decent, personable figure in broad-
cloth of the best.   For three years he kept falling
—grease coming and buttons going from the
square-skirted coat, the face puffing and pimpling,

the shoulders growing bowed, the hair falling scant and grey upon his head ; and the last that ever I saw of him, he was standing at the mouth of an entry with several men in moleskin, three parts drunk, and his old black raiment daubed with mud. I fancy that I still can hear him laugh. There was something heart-breaking in this gradual declension at so advanced an age ; you would have thought a man of sixty out of the reach of these calamities ; you would have thought that he was niched by that time into a safe place in life, whence he could pass quietly and honourably into the grave.

One of the earliest marks of these *dégringolades* is, that the victim begins to disappear from the New Town thoroughfares, and takes to the High Street, like a wounded animal to the woods. And such an one is the type of the quarter. It also has fallen socially. A scutcheon over the door somewhat jars in sentiment where there is a washing at every window. The old man, when I saw him last, wore the coat in which he had played the gentleman three years before ; and that was just what gave him so pre-eminent an air of wretchedness.

It is true that the over-population was at least as dense in the epoch of lords and ladies, and that now-a-days some customs which made Edinburgh notorious of yore have been fortunately

High Street.

pretermitted. But an aggregation of comfort is not distasteful like an aggregation of the reverse. Nobody cares how many lords and ladies, and divines and lawyers, may have been crowded

into these houses in the past—perhaps the more
the merrier. The glasses clink around the china
punch-bowl, some one touches the virginals, there
are peacocks' feathers on the chimney, and the
tapers burn clear and pale in the red firelight.
That is not an ugly picture in itself, nor will it
become ugly upon repetition. All the better
if the like were going on in every second room ;
the *land* would only look the more inviting.
Times are changed. In one house, perhaps, two-
score families herd together ; and, perhaps, not
one of them is wholly out of the reach of want.
The great hotel is given over to discomfort
from the foundation to the chimney-tops ; every-
where a pinching, narrow habit, scanty meals,
and an air of sluttishness and dirt. In the first
room there is a birth, in another a death, in a
third a sordid drinking-bout, and the detective
and the Bible-reader cross upon the stairs. High
words are audible from dwelling to dwelling,
and children have a strange experience from the
first ; only a robust soul, you would think, could
grow up in such conditions without hurt. And
even if God tempers His dispensations to the
young, and all the ill does not arise that our

apprehensions may forecast, the sight of such
a way of living is disquieting to people who are
more happily circumstanced.   Social inequality
is nowhere more ostentatious than at Edinburgh.
I have mentioned already how, to the stroller
along Princes Street, the High Street callously
exhibits its back garrets.   It is true, there is a
garden between.   And although nothing could
be more glaring by way of contrast, sometimes
the opposition is more immediate ; sometimes
the thing lies in a nutshell, and there is not so
much as a blade of grass between the rich and
poor.   To look over the South Bridge and see
the Cowgate below full of crying hawkers, is to
view one rank of society from another in the
twinkling of an eye.

One night I went along the Cowgate after
every one was a-bed but the policeman, and
stopped by hazard before a tall *land.*   The
moon touched upon its chimneys, and shone
blankly on the upper windows ; there was no
light anywhere in the great bulk of building ;
but as I stood there it seemed to me that I
could hear quite a body of quiet sounds from
the interior ; doubtless there were many clocks

ticking, and people snoring on their backs. And thus, as I fancied, the dense life within made itself faintly audible in my ears, family after family contributing its quota to the general hum, and the whole pile beating in tune to its time-pieces, like a great disordered heart. Perhaps it was little more than a fancy altogether, but it was strangely impressive at the time, and gave me an imaginative measure of the dispropor-tion between the quantity of living flesh and the trifling walls that separated and contained it.

There was nothing fanciful, at least, but every circumstance of terror and reality, in the fall of the *land* in the High Street. The building had grown rotten to the core; the entry underneath had suddenly closed up so that the scavenger's barrow could not pass; cracks and reverberations sounded through the house at night; the in-habitants of the huge old human bee-hive dis-cussed their peril when they encountered on the stair; some had even left their dwellings in a panic of fear, and returned to them again in a fit of economy or self-respect; when, in the black hours of a Sunday morning, the whole structure ran together with a hideous uproar and tumbled story upon story to the ground. The physical shock was felt far and near; and the moral shock travelled with the morning milkmaid into all the suburbs. The church-bells never sounded more dismally over Edinburgh than that grey forenoon. Death had made a brave harvest, and, like Samson, by pulling down one roof, destroyed many a home. None who saw it can have forgotten the aspect of the gable; here it was plastered, there papered, according to the rooms; here the kettle still stood on the hob, high overhead; and there a cheap picture of the Queen was pasted over the chimney. So, by this disaster, you had a glimpse into the life of thirty families, all suddenly cut off from the revolving years. The *land* had fallen; and with the *land* how much! Far in the country, people saw a gap in the city ranks, and the sun looked through between the chimneys in an unwonted place. And all over the world, in London, in Canada, in New Zealand, fancy what a multitude of people could exclaim with truth: 'The house that I was born in fell last night!'

CHAPTER III.

The Parliament Close.

TIME has wrought its changes most notably around the precincts of St. Giles's Church. The church itself, if it were not for the spire, would be unrecognisable ; the *Krames* are all gone, not a shop is left to shelter in its buttresses; and zealous magistrates and a misguided architect have shorn the design of manhood, and left it poor, naked, and pitifully pretentious. As St. Giles's must have had in former days a rich and quaint appearance now forgotten, so the neighbourhood was bustling, sunless, and romantic. It was here that the town was most overbuilt; but the overbuilding has been all rooted out, and not only a free fairway left along the High Street with an open space on either side of the church, but a great porthole, knocked in the main line of the *lands*, gives an outlook to the north and the New Town.

There is a silly story of a subterranean passage between the Castle and Holyrood, and a bold Highland piper who volunteered to explore its windings. He made his entrance by the upper end, playing a strathspey; the curious

The Spire of St. Giles's.

footed it after him down the street, following his descent by the sound of the chanter from below; until all of a sudden, about the level of St. Giles's, the music came abruptly to an end, and the people in the street stood at fault with hands uplifted. Whether he was choked with

gases, or perished in a quag, or was removed
bodily by the Evil One, remains a point of
doubt ; but the piper has never again been seen
or heard of from that day to this. Perhaps he
wandered down into the land of Thomas the
Rhymer, and some day, when it is least ex-
pected, may take a thought to revisit the sunlit
upper world. That will be a strange moment
for the cabmen on the stance besides St. Giles's,
when they hear the drone of his pipes reas-
cending from the bowels of the earth below
their horses' feet.

But it is not only pipers who have vanished,
many a solid bulk of masonry has been likewise
spirited into the air. Here, for example, is the
shape of a heart let into the causeway. This
was the site of the Tolbooth, the Heart of
Midlothian, a place old in story and namefather
to a noble book. The walls are now down in
the dust ; there is no more *squalor carceris* for
merry debtors, no more cage for the old, acknowledged prison-breaker ; but the sun and the
wind play freely over the foundations of the jail.
Nor is this the only memorial that the pavement
keeps of former days. The ancient burying-

ground of Edinburgh lay behind St. Giles's Church, running downhill to the Cowgate and covering the site of the present Parliament House. It has disappeared as utterly as the prison or the Luckenbooths ; and for those ignorant of its history, I know only one token that remains. In the Parliament Close, trodden daily underfoot by advocates, two letters and a date mark the resting-place of the man who made Scotland over again in his own image, the indefatigable, undissuadable John Knox. He sleeps within call of the church that so often echoed to his preaching.

Hard by the reformer, a bandy-legged and garlanded Charles Second, made of lead, bestrides a tun-bellied charger. The King has his backed turned, and, as you look, seems to be trotting clumsily away from such a dangerous neighbour. Often, for hours together, these two will be alone in the Close, for it lies out of the way of all but legal traffic. On one side the south wall of the church, on the other the arcades of the Parliament House, enclose this irregular bight of causeway and describe their shadows on it in the sun. At either end, from round

St. Giles's buttresses, you command a look into
the High Street with its motley passengers ; but
the stream goes by, east and west, and leaves
the Parliament Close to Charles the Second
and the birds. Once in a while, a patient
crowd may be seen loitering there all day,
some eating fruit, some reading a newspaper ;
and to judge by their quiet demeanour, you would
think they were waiting for a distribution of soup-
tickets. The fact is far otherwise ; within in the
Justiciary Court a man is upon trial for his life,
and these are some of the curious for whom the
gallery was found too narrow. Towards afternoon, if the prisoner is unpopular, there will be a
round of hisses when he is brought forth. Once
in a while, too, an advocate in wig and gown,
hand upon mouth, full of pregnant nods, sweeps
to and fro in the arcade listening to an agent ;
and at certain regular hours a whole tide of
lawyers hurries across the space.

The Parliament Close has been the scene of
marking incidents in Scottish history. Thus,
when the Bishops were ejected from the Con-
vention in 1688, 'all fourteen of them gathered
together with pale faces and stood in a cloud in

John Knox's House in the High Street.

the Parliament Close : ' poor episcopal person-
ages who were done with fair weather for life !
Some of the west-country Societarians standing
by, who would have ' rejoiced more than in
great sums ' to be at their hanging, hustled them
so rudely that they knocked their heads together.
It was not magnanimous behaviour to dethroned
enemies ; but one, at least, of the Societarians
had groaned in the *boots*, and they had all seen
their dear friends upon the scaffold.   Again, at
the 'woeful Union,' it was here that people
crowded to escort their favourite from the last of
Scottish parliaments : people flushed with nation-
ality, as Boswell would have said, ready for
riotous acts, and fresh from throwing stones at
the author of ' Robinson Crusoe' as he looked
out of window.

One of the pious in the seventeenth century,
going to pass his *trials* (examinations as we now
say) for the Scottish Bar, beheld the Parliament
Close open and had a vision of the mouth of
Hell.   This, and small wonder, was the means
of his conversion.   Nor was the vision unsuitable to the locality ; for after an hospital, what
uglier piece is there in civilisation than a court

of law? Hither come envy, malice, and all
uncharitableness to wrestle it out in public
tourney ; crimes, broken fortunes, severed households, the knave and his victim, gravitate to
this low building with the arcade. To how
many has not St. Giles's bell told the first hour
after ruin? I think I see them pause to count
the strokes, and wander on again into the
moving High Street, stunned and sick at heart.

A pair of swing doors gives admittance to a
hall with a carved roof, hung with legal por-
traits, adorned with legal statuary, lighted by
windows of painted glass, and warmed by three
vast fires. This is the *Salle des pas perdus* of
the Scottish Bar. Here, by a ferocious custom,
idle youths must promenade from ten till two.
From end to end, singly or in pairs or trios, the
gowns and wigs go back and forward. Through
a hum of talk and footfalls, the piping tones of
a Macer announce a fresh cause and call upon
the names of those concerned. Intelligent men
have been walking here daily for ten or twenty
years without a rag of business or a shilling of
reward. In process of time, they may perhaps
be made the Sheriff-Substitute and Fountain of

Justice at Lerwick or Tobermory. There is
nothing required, you would say, but a little
patience and a taste for exercise and bad air.
To breathe dust and bombazine, to feed the
mind on cackling gossip, to hear three parts of
a case and drink a glass of sherry, to long with
indescribable longings for the hour when a man
may slip out of his travesty and devote himself
to golf for the rest of the afternoon, and to
do this day by day and year after year, may
seem so small a thing to the inexperienced!
But those who have made the experiment are
of a different way of thinking, and count it the
most arduous form of idleness.

More swing doors open into pigeon-holes
where Judges of the First Appeal sit singly,
and halls of audience where the supreme Lords
sit by three or four. Here, you may see
Scott's place within the bar, where he wrote
many a page of Waverley novels to the drone
of judicial proceeding. You will hear a good
deal of shrewdness, and, as their Lordships do
not altogether disdain pleasantry, a fair proportion of dry fun. The broadest of broad Scotch
is now banished from the bench ; but the courts

still retain a certain national flavour. We have a solemn enjoyable way of lingering on a case. We treat law as a fine art, and relish and digest a good distinction. There is no hurry : point after point must be rightly examined and reduced to principle; judge after judge must utter forth his *obiter dicta* to delighted brethren.

Besides the courts, there are installed under the same roof no less than three libraries : two of no mean order; confused and semi-subterranean, full of stairs and galleries ; where you may see the most studious-looking wigs fishing out novels by lanthorn light, in the very place where the old Privy Council tortured Covenanters. As the Parliament House is built upon a slope, although it presents only one story to the north, it measures half-a-dozen at least upon the south ; and range after range of vaults extend below the libraries. Few places are more characteristic of this hilly capital. You descend one stone stair after another, and wander, by the flicker of a match, in a labyrinth of stone cellars. Now, you pass below the Outer Hall and hear overhead, brisk but ghostly, the interminable pattering of legal feet. Now, you come upon a strong door

with a wicket : on the other side are the cells
of the police office and the trap-stair that gives
admittance to the dock in the Justiciary Court.
Many a foot that has gone up there lightly
enough, has been dead-heavy in the descent.
Many a man's life has been argued away from
him during long hours in the court above. But
just now that tragic stage is empty and silent
like a church on a week-day, with the bench
all sheeted up and nothing moving but the sun-
beams on the wall. A little farther and you
strike upon a room, not empty like the rest, but
crowded with *productions* from bygone criminal
cases : a grim lumber : lethal weapons, poisoned
organs in a jar, a door with a shot-hole through
the panel, behind which a man fell dead. I
cannot fancy why they should preserve them,
unless it were against the Judgment Day. At
length, as you continue to descend, you see a
peep of yellow gaslight and hear a jostling,
whispering noise ahead ; next moment you turn
a corner, and there, in a whitewashed passage,
is a machinery belt industriously turning on its
wheels. You would think the engine had grown
there of its own accord, like a cellar fungus, and

would soon spin itself out and fill the vaults from
end to end with its mysterious labours.   In truth,
it is only some gear of the steam ventilator ; and
you will find the engineers at hand, and may
step out of their door into the sunlight.   For all
this while, you have not been descending towards the earth's centre, but only to the bottom
of the hill and the foundations of the Parliament
House ; low down, to be sure, but still under
the open heaven and in a field of grass.   The
daylight shines garishly on the back windows of
the Irish quarter ; on broken shutters, wry
gables, old palsied houses on the brink of ruin,
a crumbling human pig-sty fit for human pigs.
There are few signs of life, besides a scanty
washing or a face at a window : the dwellers are
abroad, but they will return at night and stagger
to their pallets.

CHAPTER IV.

Legends.

THE character of a place is often most perfectly expressed in its associations. An event strikes root and grows into a legend, when it has happened amongst congenial surroundings. Ugly actions, above all in ugly places, have the true romantic quality, and become an undying property of their scene. To a man like Scott, the different appearances of nature seemed each to contain its own legend ready made, which it was his to call forth : in such or such a place, only such or such events ought with propriety to happen ; and in this spirit he made the *Lady of the Lake* for Ben Venue, the *Heart of Midlothian* for Edinburgh, and the *Pirate*, so indifferently written but so romantically conceived, for the desolate islands and roaring tideways of the North. The common run of mankind have, from generation to generation, an instinct almost as delicate as

that of Scott ; but where he created new things,
they only forget what is unsuitable among the
old ; and by survival of the fittest, a body of
tradition becomes a work of art.   So, in the
low dens and high-flying garrets of Edinburgh,
people may go back upon dark passages in the
town's adventures, and chill their marrow with
winter's tales about the fire : tales that are
singularly apposite and characteristic, not only
of the old life, but of the very constitution of
built nature in that part, and singularly well
qualified to add horror to horror, when the
wind pipes around the tall *lands*, and hoots
adown arched passages, and the far-spread wil-
derness of city lamps keeps quavering and flaring
in the gusts.

Here, it is the tale of Begbie the bank-porter,
stricken to the heart at a blow and left in his
blood within a step or two of the crowded High
Street.   There, people hush their voices over
Burke and Hare ; over drugs and violated
graves, and the resurrection-men smothering
their victims with their knees.   Here, again, the
fame of Deacon Brodie is kept piously fresh.
A great man in his day was the Deacon ; well

seen in good society, crafty with his hands as a
cabinet-maker, and one who could sing a song
with taste. Many a citizen was proud to wel-
come the Deacon to supper, and dismissed him

The Canongate.

with regret at a timeous hour, who would have
been vastly disconcerted had he known how soon,
and in what guise, his visitor returned. Many
stories are told of this redoubtable Edinburgh
burglar, but the one I have in my mind most
vividly gives the key of all the rest. A friend

of Brodie's, nested some way towards heaven in
one of these great *lands*, had told him of a pro-
jected visit to the country, and afterwards, de-
tained by some affairs, put it off and stayed the
night in town.   The good man had lain some
time awake ; it was far on in the small hours by
the Tron bell ; when suddenly there came a
creak, a jar, a faint light.   Softly he clambered
out of bed and up to a false window which looked
upon another room, and there, by the glimmer
of a thieves' lantern, was his good friend the
Deacon in a mask.   It is characteristic of the
town and the town's manners that this little
episode should have been quietly tided over,
and quite a good time elapsed before a great
robbery, an escape, a Bow Street runner, a cock-
fight, an apprehension in a cupboard in Amster-
dam, and a last step into the air off his own
greatly-improved gallows drop, brought the career
of Deacon William Brodie to an end.   But still,
by the mind's eye, he may be seen, a man
harassed below a mountain of duplicity, slinking
from a magistrate's supper - room to a thieves'
ken, and pickeering among the closes by the
flicker of a dark lamp.

Planestones Close, Canongate.

Or where the Deacon is out of favour, perhaps some memory lingers of the great plagues, and of fatal houses still unsafe to enter within the memory of man.   For in time of pestilence the discipline had been sharp and sudden, and what we now call 'stamping out contagion' was carried on with deadly rigour.   The officials, in their gowns of grey, with a white St. Andrew's cross on back and breast, and a white cloth carried before them on a staff, perambulated the city, adding the terror of man's justice to the fear of God's visitation.   The dead they buried on the Borough Muir ; the living who had concealed the sickness were drowned, if they were women, in the Quarry Holes, and if they were men, were hanged and gibbeted at their own doors ; and wherever the evil had passed, furniture was destroyed and houses closed.   And the most bogeyish part of the story is about such houses.   Two generations back they still stood dark and empty ; people avoided them as they passed by ; the boldest schoolboy only shouted through the keyhole and made off ; for within, it was supposed, the plague lay ambushed like a basilisk, ready to flow forth and spread blain and pustule through the city. What a terrible next-door neighbour for superstitious citizens! A rat scampering within would send a shudder through the stoutest heart. Here, if you like, was a sanitary parable, addressed by our uncleanly forefathers to their own neglect.

And then we have Major Weir; for although even his house is now demolished, old Edinburgh cannot clear herself of his unholy memory. He and his sister lived together in an odour of sour piety. She was a marvellous spinster; he had a rare gift of supplication, and was known among devout admirers by the name of Angelical Thomas. 'He was a tall, black man, and ordinarily looked down to the ground; a grim countenance, and a big nose. His garb was still a cloak, and somewhat dark, and he never went without his staff.' How it came about that Angelical Thomas was burned in company with his staff, and his sister in gentler manner hanged, and whether these two were simply religious maniacs of the more furious order, or had real as well as imaginary sins upon their old-world shoulders, are points happily beyond the reach of our intention. At least, it is suitable enough that out of this superstitious city some such example should have been put forth : the outcome and fine flower of dark and vehement religion. And at least the facts struck the public fancy and brought forth a remarkable family of myths. It would appear that the Major's staff went upon his errands, and even ran before him with a lantern on dark nights. Gigantic females, 'stentoriously laughing and gaping with tehees of laughter' at unseasonable hours of night and morning, haunted the purlieus of his abode. His house fell under such a load of infamy that no one dared to sleep in it, until municipal improvement levelled the structure to the ground. And my father has often been told in the nursery how the devil's coach, drawn by six coal-black horses with fiery eyes, would drive at night into the West Bow, and belated people might see the dead Major through the glasses.

Another legend is that of the two maiden sisters. A legend I am afraid it may be, in the most discreditable meaning of the term ; or perhaps something worse—a mere yesterday's fiction. But it is a story of some vitality, and is worthy of a place in the Edinburgh kalendar. This pair inhabited a single room ; from the facts, it must have been double-bedded ; and it may have been of some dimensions : but when all is said, it was a single room.   Here our two spinsters fell out —on some point of controversial divinity belike : but fell out so bitterly that there was never a word spoken between them, black or white, from that day forward.   You would have thought they would separate : but no ; whether from lack of means, or the Scottish fear of scandal, they continued to keep house together where they were. A chalk line drawn upon the floor separated their two domains ; it bisected the doorway and the fireplace, so that each could go out and in, and do her cooking, without violating the territory of the other.   So, for years, they coexisted in a hateful silence ; their meals, their ablutions, their friendly visitors, exposed to an unfriendly scrutiny ; and at night, in the dark watches, each could hear the breathing of her enemy.   Never did four walls look down upon an uglier spectacle than these sisters rivalling in unsisterliness. Here is a canvas for Hawthorne to have turned into a cabinet picture—he had a Puritanic vein, which would have fitted him to treat this Puritanic horror ; he could have shown them to us in their sicknesses and at their hideous twin de-

votions, thumbing a pair of great Bibles, or pray-
ing aloud for each other's penitence with marrowy
emphasis; now each, with kilted petticoat, at her
own corner of the fire on some tempestuous evening; now sitting each at her window, looking out
upon the summer landscape sloping far below
them towards the firth, and the field-paths where
they had wandered hand in hand; or, as age and
infirmity grew upon them and prolonged their
toilettes, and their hands began to tremble and
their heads to nod involuntarily, growing only
the more steeled in enmity with years; until one
fine day, at a word, a look, a visit, or the approach of death, their hearts would melt and the
chalk boundary be overstepped for ever.

Alas! to those who know the ecclesiastical
history of the race—the most perverse and melancholy in man's annals—this will seem only a
figure of much that is typical of Scotland and
her high-seated capital above the Forth—a figure
so grimly realistic that it may pass with strangers
for a caricature. We are wonderful patient haters
for conscience sake up here in the North. I
spoke, in the first of these papers, of the Parliaments of the Established and Free Churches, and
how they can hear each other singing psalms

across the street. There is but a street between
them in space, but a shadow between them in
principle ; and yet there they sit, enchanted, and
in damnatory accents pray for each other's growth
in grace. It would be well if there were no
more than two ; but the sects in Scotland form
a large family of sisters, and the chalk lines are
thickly drawn, and run through the midst of
many private homes. Edinburgh is a city of
churches, as though it were a place of pilgrimage.
You will see four within a stone-cast at the head
of the West Bow. Some are crowded to the
doors ; some are empty like monuments ; and yet
you will ever find new ones in the building.
Hence that surprising clamour of church bells
that suddenly breaks out upon the Sabbath morning from Trinity and the sea-skirts to Morningside on the borders of the hills. I have heard
the chimes of Oxford playing their symphony in
a golden autumn morning, and beautiful it was
to hear. But in. Edinburgh all manner of loud
bells join, or rather disjoin, in one swelling, brutal
babblement of noise. Now one overtakes another,
and now lags behind it ; now five or six all strike
on the pained tympanum at the same punctual
instant of time, and make together a dismal chord

of discord ; and now for a second all seem to have conspired to hold their peace. Indeed, there are not many uproars in this world more dismal than that of the Sabbath bells in Edinburgh : a harsh ecclesiastical tocsin ; the outcry of incongruous orthodoxies, calling on every separate conventicler to put up a protest, each in his own synagogue, against 'right-hand extremes and left-hand defections.' And surely there are few worse extremes than this extremity of zeal ; and few more deplorable defections than this disloyalty to Christian love. Shakespeare wrote a comedy of 'Much Ado about Nothing.' The Scottish nation made a fantastic tragedy on the same subject. And it is for the success of this remarkable piece that these bells are sounded every Sabbath morning on the hills above the Forth. How many of them might rest silent in the steeple, how many of these ugly churches might be demolished and turned once more into useful building material, if people who think almost exactly the same thoughts about religion would condescend to worship God under the same roof ! But there are the chalk lines. And which is to pocket pride, and speak the foremost word ?

CHAPTER V.

Greyfriars.

I T was Queen Mary who threw open the gardens of the Grey Friars : a new and semi-rural cemetery in those days, although it has grown an antiquity in its turn and been superseded by half-a-dozen others. The Friars must have had a pleasant time on summer evenings ; for their gardens were situated to a wish, with the tall castle and the tallest of the castle crags in front. Even now, it is one of our famous Edinburgh points of view ; and strangers are led thither to see, by yet another instance, how strangely the city lies upon her hills. The enclosure is of an irregular shape ; the double church of Old and New Greyfriars stands on the level at the top ; a few thorns are dotted here and there, and the ground falls by terrace and steep slope towards the north. The open shows many slabs and table tombstones ; and all round the margin, the place is girt by an array of aristocratic mausoleums appallingly adorned.

Setting aside the tombs of Roubiliac, which belong to the heroic order of graveyard art, **we** Scotch stand, to my fancy, highest among nations in the matter of grimly illustrating death. We seem to love for their own sake the emblems of time and the great change; and even around country churches you will find a wonderful exhibition of skulls, and crossbones, and noseless angels, and trumpets pealing for the Judgment Day. Every mason was a pedestrian Holbein: he had a deep consciousness of death, and loved to put its terrors pithily before the churchyard loiterer; he was brimful of rough hints upon mortality, and any dead farmer was seized upon to be a text. The classical examples of this art are in Greyfriars. In their time, these were doubtless costly monuments, and reckoned of a very elegant proportion by contemporaries; and now, when the elegance is not so apparent, the significance remains. You may perhaps look with a smile on the profusion of Latin mottoes —some crawling endwise up the shaft of a pillar, some issuing on a scroll from angels' trumpets—

on the emblematic horrors, the figures rising
headless from the grave, and all the traditional
ingenuities in which it pleased our fathers to set
forth their sorrow for the dead and their sense
of earthly mutability. But it is not a hearty sort
of mirth. Each ornament may have been executed by the merriest apprentice, whistling as he
plied the mallet ; but the original meaning of
each, and the combined effect of so many of them
in this quiet enclosure, is serious to the point of
melancholy.

Round a great part of the circuit, houses of
a low class present their backs to the churchyard. Only a few inches separate the living
from the dead. Here, a window is partly blocked
up by the pediment of a tomb ; there, where the
street falls far below the level of the graves, a
chimney has been trained up the back of a
monument, and a red pot looks vulgarly over
from behind. A damp smell of the graveyard
finds its way into houses where workmen sit at
meat. Domestic life on a small scale goes forward
visibly at the windows. The very solitude and
stillness of the enclosure, which lies apart from
the town's traffic, serves to accentuate the con-

trast.   As you walk upon the graves, you see children scattering crumbs to feed the sparrows ; you hear people singing or washing dishes, or the sound of tears and castigation ; the linen on a clothes-pole flaps against funereal sculpture ; or perhaps the cat slips over the lintel and descends on a memorial urn.   And as there is nothing else astir, these incongruous sights and noises take hold on the attention and exaggerate the sadness of the place.

Greyfriars is continually overrun by cats.   I have seen one afternoon, as many as thirteen of them seated on the grass beside old Milne, the Master Builder, all sleek and fat, and complacently blinking, as if they had fed upon strange meats.   Old Milne was chaunting with the saints, as we may hope, and cared little for the company about his grave ; but I confess the spectacle had an ugly side for me ; and I was glad to step forward and raise my eyes to where the Castle and the roofs of the Old Town, and the spire of the Assembly Hall, stood deployed against the sky with the colourless precision of engraving.   An open outlook is to be desired from a churchyard, and a sight of the sky and

Greyfriars.

some of the world's beauty relieves a mind from morbid thoughts.

I shall never forget one visit. It was a grey, dropping day ; the grass was strung with rain-drops ; and the people in the houses kept hanging out their shirts and petticoats and angrily taking them in again, as the weather turned from wet to fair and back again. A grave-digger, and a friend of his, a gardener from the country, accompanied me into one after another of the cells and little courtyards in which it gratified the wealthy of old days to enclose their old bones from neighbourhood. In one, under a sort of shrine, we found a forlorn human effigy, very realistically executed down to the detail of his ribbed stockings, and holding in his hand a ticket with the date of his demise. He looked most pitiful and ridiculous, shut up by himself in his aristocratic precinct, like a bad old boy or an inferior forgotten deity under a new dispensation ; the burdocks grew familiarly about his feet, the rain dripped all round him ; and the world maintained the most entire indifference as to who he was or whither he had gone. In another, a vaulted tomb, handsome externally but horrible inside with damp and cobwebs, there were three mounds of black earth and an un- covered thigh bone. This was the place of interment, it appeared, of a family with whom the gardener had been long in service. He was among old acquaintances. 'This'll be Miss Marg'et's,' said he, giving the bone a friendly kick. ' The auld —— ! ' I have always an un- comfortable feeling in a graveyard, at sight of so many tombs to perpetuate memories best for- gotten ; but I never had the impression so strongly as that day. People had been at some expense in both these cases : to provoke a melancholy feeling of derision in the one, and an insulting epithet in the other. The proper inscription for the most part of mankind, I began to think, is the cynical jeer, *cras tibi*. That, if anything, will stop the mouth of a carper ; since it both admits the worst and carries the war triumphantly into the enemy's camp.

Greyfriars is a place of many associations. There was one window in a house at the lower end, now demolished, which was pointed out to me by the gravedigger as a spot of legendary interest. Burke, the resurrection man, infamous

for so many murders at five shillings a-head, used
to sit thereat, with pipe and nightcap, to watch
burials going forward on the green. In a tomb
higher up, which must then have been but newly
finished, John Knox, according to the same in-
formant, had taken refuge in a turmoil of the
Reformation. Behind the church is the haunted
mausoleum of Sir George Mackenzie : Bloody
Mackenzie, Lord Advocate in the Covenanting
troubles and author of some pleasing sentiments
on toleration. Here, in the last century, an old
Heriot's Hospital boy once harboured from the
pursuit of the police. The Hospital is next door
to Greyfriars — a courtly building among lawns,
where, on Founder's Day, you may see a multitude
of children playing Kiss-in-the-Ring and Round
the Mulberry-bush. Thus, when the fugitive had
managed to conceal himself in the tomb, his old
schoolmates had a hundred opportunities to bring
him food ; and there he lay in safety till a ship
was found to smuggle him abroad. But his must
have been indeed a heart of brass, to lie all day
and night alone with the dead persecutor ; and
other lads were far from emulating him in courage.
When a man's soul is certainly in hell, his body

will scarce lie quiet in a tomb however costly;
some time or other the door must open, and the
reprobate come forth in the abhorred garments
of the grave. It was thought a high piece of
prowess to knock at the Lord Advocate's mausoleum and challenge him to appear. 'Bluidy
Mackingie, come oot if ye dar'!' sang the fool-
hardy urchins. But Sir George had other affairs
on hand; and the author of an essay on toleration
continues to sleep peacefully among the many
whom he so intolerantly helped to slay.

For this *infelix campus*, as it is dubbed in one
of its own inscriptions—an inscription over which
Dr. Johnson passed a critical eye—is in many
ways sacred to the memory of the men whom
Mackenzie persecuted. It was here, on the flat
tombstones, that the Covenant was signed by an
enthusiastic people. In the long arm of the churchyard that extends to Lauriston, the prisoners from
Bothwell Bridge—fed on bread and water and
guarded, life for life, by vigilant marksmen—lay
five months looking for the scaffold or the plantations. And while the good work was going forward in the Grassmarket, idlers in Greyfriars
might have heard the throb of the military drums

that drowned the voices of the martyrs. Nor is this all : for down in the corner farthest from Sir George, there stands a monument dedicated, in uncouth Covenanting verse, to all who lost their

The Grassmarket.

lives in that contention. There is no moorsman shot in a snow shower beside Irongray or Co'monell; there is not one of the two hundred who were drowned off the Orkneys; nor so much as a poor, over-driven, Covenanting slave in the American plantations; but can lay claim to a share in that memorial, and, if such things interest just men among the shades, can boast he has a monument on earth as well as Julius Cæsar or the Pharaohs. Where they may all lie, I know not. Far-scattered bones, indeed! But if the reader cares to learn how some of them—or some part of some of them—found their way at length to such honourable sepulture, let him listen to the words of one who was their comrade in life and their apologist when they were dead. Some of the insane controversial matter I omit, as well as some digressions, but leave the rest in Patrick Walker's language and orthography :—

'The never to be forgotten Mr. *James Renwick* told me, that he was Witness to their Public Murder at the *Gallowlee*, between *Leith* and *Edinburgh*, when he saw the Hangman hash and hagg off all their Five Heads, with *Patrick Foreman's* Right Hand : Their Bodies were all buried at the Gallows Foot ; their Heads, with *Patrick's* Hand, were brought and put upon five Pikes on the *Pleasaunce-Port.* . . . Mr. *Renwick* told me also that it was the first public Action that his Hand was at, to conveen Friends, and lift their murthered Bodies, and carried them to the West Churchyard of *Edinburgh*,'—not Greyfriars, this time,— 'and buried them there. Then they came about the

City . . . . and took down these Five Heads and that
Hand; and Day being come, they went quickly up
the *Pleasaunce;* and when they came to *Lauristoun*
Yards, upon the South-side of the City, they durst
not venture, being so light, to go and bury their
Heads with their Bodies, which they designed; it
being present Death, if any of them had been found.
Alexander Tweedie, a Friend, being with them, who at
that Time was Gardner in these Yards, concluded to
bury them in his Yard, being in a Box (wrapped in
Linen), where they lay 45 Years except 3 Days, being
executed upon the 10th of *October* 1681, and found the
7th Day of *October* 1726. That Piece of Ground lay
for some Years unlaboured; and trenching it, the
Gardner found them, which affrighted him; the Box
was consumed.   Mr. *Schaw*, the Owner of these Yards,
caused lift them, and lay them upon a Table in his
Summer-house : Mr. *Schaw's* mother was so kind, as
to cut out a Linen-cloth, and cover them.   They lay
Twelve Days there, where all had Access to see them.
Alexander Tweedie, the foresaid Gardner, said, when
dying, There was a Treasure hid in his Yard, but
neither Gold nor Silver.   *Daniel Tweedie*, his Son,
came along with me to that Yard, and told me that
his Father planted a white Rose-bush above them, and
farther down the Yard a red Rose-bush, which were
more fruitful than any other Bush in the Yard. . . .
Many came '— to see the heads —' out of Curiosity;
yet I rejoiced to see so many concerned grave Men

and Women favouring the Dust of our Martyrs. There were Six of us concluded to bury them upon the Nineteenth Day of *October* 1726, and every One of us to acquaint Friends of the Day and Hour, being *Wednesday*, the Day of the Week on which most of them were executed, and at 4 of the Clock at Night, being the Hour that most of them went to their resting Graves. We caused make a compleat Coffin for them in Black, with four Yards of fine Linen, the way that our Martyrs Corps were managed. . . . Accordingly we kept the aforesaid Day and Hour, and doubled the Linen, and laid the Half of it below them, their nether Jaws being parted from their Heads; but being young Men, their Teeth remained. All were Witness to the Holes in each of their Heads, which the Hangman broke with his Hammer; and according to the Bigness of their Sculls, we laid the Jaws to them, and drew the other Half of the Linen above them, and stufft the Coffin with Shavings. Some prest hard to go thorow the chief Parts of the City as was done at the Revolution; but this we refused, considering that it looked airy and frothy, to make such Show of them, and inconsistent with the solid serious Observing of such an affecting, surprizing unheard-of Dispensation : But took the ordinary Way of other Burials from that Place, to wit, we went east the Back of the Wall, and in at *Bristo-Port*, and down the Way to the Head of the *Cowgate*, and turned up to the Church-yard, where they were interred closs to the Martyrs Tomb, with the

greatest Multitude of People Old and Young, Men
and Women, Ministers and others, that ever I saw
together.'

And so there they were at last, in 'their resting graves.' So long as men do their duty, even
if it be greatly in a misapprehension, they will
be leading pattern lives ; and whether or not they
come to lie beside a martyrs' monument, we may
be sure they will find a safe haven somewhere
in the providence of God. It is not well to think
of death, unless we temper the thought with that
of heroes who despised it. Upon what ground,
is of small account ; if it be only the bishop who
was burned for his faith in the antipodes, his
memory lightens the heart and makes us walk
undisturbed among graves. And so the martyrs'
monument is a wholesome, heartsome spot in the
field of the dead ; and as we look upon it, a brave
influence comes to us from the land of those who
have won their discharge and, in another phrase
of Patrick Walker's, got 'cleanly off the stage.'

CHAPTER VI.

New Town—Town and Country.

IT is as much a matter of course to decry
the New Town as to exalt the Old; and
the most celebrated authorities have picked out
this quarter as the very emblem of what is con-
demnable in architecture. Much may be said,
much indeed has been said, upon the text;
but to the unsophisticated, who call anything
pleasing if it only pleases them, the New Town
of Edinburgh seems, in itself, not only gay and
airy, but highly picturesque. An old skipper,
invincibly ignorant of all theories of the sublime
and beautiful, once propounded as his most
radiant notion for Paradise: 'The new town of
Edinburgh, with the wind a matter of a point
free.' He has now gone to that sphere where
all good tars are promised pleasant weather in
the song, and perhaps his thoughts fly somewhat higher. But there are bright and temperate
days—with soft air coming from the inland hills,

military music sounding bravely from the hollow of the gardens, the flags all waving on the palaces of Princes Street—when I have seen the town through a sort of glory, and shaken hands in sentiment with the old sailor. And indeed, for a man who has been much tumbled round Orcadian skerries, what scene could be more agreeable to witness? On such a day, the valley wears a surprising air of festival. It seems (I do not know how else to put my meaning) as if it were a trifle too good to be true. It is what Paris ought to be. It has the scenic quality that would best set off a life of unthinking, open-air diversion. It was meant by nature for the realisation of the society of comic operas. And you can imagine, if the climate were but towardly, how all the world and his wife would flock into these gardens in the cool of the evening, to hear cheerful music, to sip pleasant drinks, to see the moon rise from behind Arthur's Seat and shine upon the spires and monuments and the green tree-tops in the valley. Alas! and the next morning the rain is splashing on the windows, and the passengers flee along Princes Street before the galloping squalls.

It cannot be denied that the original design
was faulty and short-sighted, and did not fully
profit by the capabilities of the situation. The
architect was essentially a town bird, and he
laid out the modern city with a view to street

The Royal Institution.

scenery, and to street scenery alone. The country
did not enter into his plan ; he had never lifted
his eyes to the hills. If he had so chosen, every
street upon the northern slope might have been
a noble terrace and commanded an extensive
and beautiful view. But the space has been too
closely built ; many of the houses front the

wrong way, intent, like the Man with the Muck-Rake, on what is not worth observation, and standing discourteously back-foremost in the ranks; and, in a word, it is too often only from attic-windows, or here and there at a crossing, that you can get a look beyond the city upon its diversified surroundings. But perhaps it is all the more surprising, to come suddenly on a corner, and see a perspective of a mile or more of falling street, and beyond that woods and villas, and a blue arm of sea, and the hills upon the farther side.

Fergusson, our Edinburgh poet, Burns's model, once saw a butterfly at the Town Cross; and the sight inspired him with a worthless little ode. This painted country man, the dandy of the rose garden, looked far abroad in such a humming neighbourhood; and you can fancy what moral considerations a youthful poet would supply. But the incident, in a fanciful sort of way, is characteristic of the place. Into no other city does the sight of the country enter so far; if you do not meet a butterfly, you shall certainly catch a glimpse of far-away trees upon your walk; and the place is full of theatre tricks in the way of scenery. You peep under an arch, you descend stairs that look as if they would land you in a cellar, you turn to the back-window of a grimy tenement in a lane: — and behold! you are face-to-face with distant and bright prospects. You turn a corner, and there is the sun going down into the Highland hills. You look down an alley, and see ships tacking for the Baltic.

For the country people to see Edinburgh on her hill-tops, is one thing; it is another for the citizen, from the thick of his affairs, to overlook the country. It should be a genial and ameliorating influence in life; it should prompt good thoughts and remind him of Nature's unconcern: that he can watch from day to day, as he trots officeward, how the Spring green brightens in the wood or the field grows black under a moving ploughshare. I have been tempted, in this connexion, to deplore the slender faculties of the human race, with its penny-whistle of a voice, its dull ears, and its narrow range of sight. If you could see as people are to see in heaven, if you had eyes such as you can fancy for a superior race, if you could take clear note of

the objects of vision, not only a few yards, but
a few miles from where you stand :—think how
agreeably your sight would be entertained, how
pleasantly your thoughts would be diversified,
as you walked the Edinburgh streets! For you
might pause, in some business perplexity, in the
midst of the city traffic, and perhaps catch the
eye of a shepherd as he sat down to breathe
upon a heathery shoulder of the Pentlands ; or
perhaps some urchin, clambering in a country
elm, would put aside the leaves and show you
his flushed and rustic visage ; or a fisher racing
seawards, with the tiller under his elbow, and
the sail sounding in the wind, would fling
you a salutation from between Anst'er and the
May.

To be old is not the same thing as to be
picturesque ; nor because the Old Town bears a
strange physiognomy, does it at all follow that
the New Town shall look commonplace. Indeed, apart from antique houses, it is curious
how much description would apply commonly
to either. The same sudden accidents of ground,
a similar dominating site above the plain, and
the same superposition of one rank of society

over another, are to be observed in both. Thus, the broad and comely approach to Princes Street from the east, lined with hotels and public offices, makes a leap over the gorge of the Low Calton ; if you cast a glance over the parapet, you look direct into that sunless and disreputable confluent of Leith Street ; and the same tall houses open upon both thoroughfares. This is only the New Town passing overhead above its own cellars; walking, so to speak, over its own children, as is the way of cities and the human race. But at the Dean Bridge, you may behold a spectacle of a more novel order. The river runs at the bottom of a deep valley, among rocks and between gardens; the crest of either bank is occupied by some of the most commodious streets and crescents in the modern city ; and a handsome bridge unites the two summits. Over this, every afternoon, private carriages go spinning by, and ladies with card-cases pass to and fro about the duties of society. And yet down below, you may still see, with its mills and foaming weir, the little rural village of Dean. Modern improvement has gone overhead on its high-level viaduct ; and the extended city has cleanly overleapt, and left unaltered, what was once the summer retreat of its comfortable citizens. Every town embraces hamlets in its growth; Edinburgh herself has embraced a good few; but it is strange to see one still surviving—and to see it some hundreds of feet below your path. Is it Torre del Greco that is built above buried Herculaneum? Herculaneum was dead at least; but the sun still shines upon the roofs of Dean; the smoke still rises thriftily from its chimneys; the dusty miller comes to his door, looks at the gurgling water, hearkens to the turning wheel and the birds about the shed, and perhaps whistles an air of his own to enrich the symphony — for all the world as if Edinburgh were still the old Edinburgh on the Castle Hill, and Dean were still the quietest of hamlets buried a mile or so in the green country.

It is not so long ago since magisterial David Hume lent the authority of his example to the exodus from the Old Town, and took up his new abode in a street which is still (so oddly may a jest become perpetuated) known as Saint David Street. Nor is the town so large but a holiday schoolboy may harry a bird's nest within

In the Village of Dean.

half a mile of his own door. There are places
that still smell of the plough in memory's nostrils.
Here, one had heard a blackbird on a hawthorn;
there, another was taken on summer evenings to
eat strawberries and cream ; and you have seen
a waving wheatfield on the site of your present
residence. The memories of an Edinburgh boy
are but partly memories of the town. I look
back with delight on many an escalade of garden
walls ; many a ramble among lilacs full of piping
birds ; many an exploration in obscure quarters
that were neither town nor country ; and I think
that both for my companions and myself, there
was a special interest, a point of romance, and
a sentiment as of foreign travel, when we hit in
our excursions on the butt-end of some former
hamlet, and found a few rustic cottages em-
bedded among streets and squares. The tunnel
to the Scotland Street Station, the sight of the
trains shooting out of its dark maw with the two
guards upon the brake, the thought of its length
and the many ponderous edifices and open
thoroughfares above, were certainly things of
paramount impressiveness to a young mind. It
was a subterranean passage, although of a larger
bore than we were accustomed to in Ainsworth's

novels ; and these two words, ' subterreanean
passage,' were in themselves an irresistible attraction, and seemed to bring us nearer in spirit to
the heroes we loved and the black rascals we
secretly aspired to imitate. To scale the Castle
Rock from West Princes Street Gardens, and
lay a triumphal hand against the rampart itself,
was to taste a high order of romantic pleasure.
And there are other sights and exploits which
crowd back upon my mind under a very strong
illumination of remembered pleasure. But the
effect of not one of them all will compare with
the discoverer's joy, and the sense of old Time and
his slow changes on the face of this earth, with
which I explored such corners as Cannonmills
or Water Lane, or the nugget of cottages at
Broughton Market. They were more rural than
the open country, and gave a greater impression
of antiquity than the oldest *land* upon the High
Street. They too, like Fergusson's butterfly, had
a quaint air of having wandered far from their
own place ; they looked abashed and homely,
with their gables and their creeping plants, their
outside stairs and running mill-streams ; there
were corners that smelt like the end of the
country garden where I spent my Aprils ; and

the people stood to gossip at their doors, as they might have done in Colinton or Cramond.

In a great measure we may, and shall, eradicate this haunting flavour of the country. The last elm is dead in Elm Row; and the villas and the workmen's quarters spread apace on all the borders of the city. We can cut down the trees; we can bury the grass under dead paving-stones; we can drive brisk streets through all our sleepy quarters; and we may forget the stories and the playgrounds of our boyhood. But we have some possessions that not even the infuriate zeal of builders can utterly abolish and destroy. Nothing can abolish the hills, unless it be a cataclysm of nature which shall subvert Edinburgh Castle itself and lay all her florid structures in the dust. And as long as we have the hills and the Firth, we have a famous heritage to leave our children. Our windows, at no expense to us, are most artfully stained to represent a landscape. And when the Spring comes round, and the hawthorns begin to flower, and the meadows to smell of young grass, even in the thickest of our streets, the country hilltops find out a young man's eyes, and set his heart beating for travel and pure air.

CHAPTER VII.

The Villa Quarters.

MR. RUSKIN'S denunciation of the New Town of Edinburgh includes, as I have heard it repeated, nearly all the stone and lime we have to show. Many however find a grand air and something settled and imposing in the better parts ; and upon many, as I have said, the confusion of styles induces an agreeable stimulation of the mind. But upon the subject of our recent villa architecture, I am frankly ready to mingle my tears with Mr. Ruskin's, and it is a subject which makes one envious of his large declamatory and controversial eloquence.

Day by day, one new villa, one new object of offence, is added to another ; all around New-ington and Morningside, the dismallest structures keep springing up like mushrooms ; the pleasant hills are loaded with them, each impudently squatted in its garden, each roofed and carrying chimneys like a house. And yet a glance of an eye discovers their true character. They are not houses ; for they were not designed with a view to human habitation, and the internal arrangements are, as they tell me, fantastically unsuited to the needs of man. They are not buildings ; for you can scarcely say a thing is built where every measurement is in clamant disproportion with its neighbour. They belong to no style of art, only to a form of business much to be regretted.

Why should it be cheaper to erect a structure where the size of the windows bears no rational relation to the size of the front ? Is there any profit in a misplaced chimney-stalk ? Does a hard-working, greedy builder gain more on a monstrosity than on a decent cottage of equal plainness ? Frankly, we should say, No. Bricks may be omitted, and green timber employed, in the construction of even a very elegant design ; and there is no reason why a chimney should be made to vent, because it is so situated as to look comely from without. On the other hand, there is a noble way of being ugly: a high-aspiring fiasco like the fall of Lucifer. There are daring and gaudy buildings that manage to be offensive,

without being contemptible ; and we know that
'fools rush in where angels fear to tread.' But
to aim at making a common-place villa, and to
make it insufferably ugly in each particular ; to
attempt the homeliest achievement, and to attain
the bottom of derided failure ; not to have any
theory but profit and yet, at an equal expense,
to outstrip all competitors in the art of conceiving
and rendering permanent deformity ; and to do
all this in what is, by nature, one of the most
agreeable neighbourhoods in Britain : — what are
we to say, but that this also is a distinction, hard
to earn although not greatly worshipful ?

Indifferent buildings give pain to the sensi-
tive ; but these things offend the plainest taste.
It is a danger which threatens the amenity of
the town ; and as this eruption keeps spreading
on our borders, we have ever the farther to walk
among unpleasant sights, before we gain the
country air. If the population of Edinburgh
were a living, autonomous body, it would arise
like one man and make night hideous with arson ;
the builders and their accomplices would be
driven to work, like the Jews of yore, with the
trowel in one hand and the defensive cutlass in

the other; and as soon as one of these masonic
wonders had been consummated, right-minded
iconoclasts should fall thereon and make an end
of it at once.

Possibly these words may meet the eye of a
builder or two. It is no use asking them to em-
ploy an architect; for that would be to touch
them in a delicate quarter, and its use would
largely depend on what architect they were
minded to call in. But let them get any architect in the world to point out any reasonably
well-proportioned villa, not his own design; and
let them reproduce that model to satiety.

CHAPTER VIII.

The Calton Hill.

THE east of new Edinburgh is guarded
by a craggy hill, of no great elevation,
which the town embraces. The old London
road runs on one side of it; while the New
Approach, leaving it on the other hand, com-
pletes the circuit. You mount by stairs in a
cutting of the rock to find yourself in a field
of monuments. Dugald Stewart has the honours
of situation and architecture; Burns is memo-
rialised lower down upon a spur; Lord Nelson,
as befits a sailor, gives his name to the top-
gallant of the Calton Hill. This latter erection
has been differently and yet, in both cases,
aptly compared to a telescope and a butter-
churn; comparisons apart, it ranks among the
vilest of men's handiworks. But the chief
feature is an unfinished range of columns,
'the Modern Ruin' as it has been called, an
imposing object from far and near, and giving

Edinburgh, even from the sea, that false air of a Modern Athens which has earned for her so many slighting speeches. It was meant to be a National Monument; and its present state is a very suitable monument to certain national characteristics. The old Observatory— a quaint brown building on the edge of the

The Calton Hill.

steep—and the new Observatory—a classical edifice with a dome—occupy the central portion of the summit. All these are scattered on a green turf, browsed over by some sheep.

The scene suggests reflections on fame and on man's injustice to the dead. You see Dugald Stewart rather more handsomely commemorated than Burns. Immediately below, in the Canongate churchyard, lies Robert

Fergusson, Burns's master in his art, who died insane while yet a stripling ; and if Dugald Stewart has been somewhat too boisterously acclaimed, the Edinburgh poet, on the other hand, is most unrighteously forgotten. The votaries of Burns, a crew too common in all ranks in Scotland and more remarkable for number than discretion, eagerly suppress all mention of the lad who handed to him the poetic impulse and, up to the time when he grew famous, continued to influence him in his manner and the choice of subjects. Burns himself not only acknowledged his debt in a fragment of autobiography, but erected a tomb over the grave in Canongate churchyard. This was worthy of an artist, but it was done in vain ; and although I think I have read nearly all the biographies of Burns, I cannot remember one in which the modesty of nature was not violated, or where Fergusson was not sacrificed to the credit of his follower's originality. There is a kind of gaping admiration that would fain roll Shakespeare and Bacon into one, to have a bigger thing to gape at ; and a class of men who cannot edit one author without disparaging all others. They are indeed mistaken if they think to please the great originals; and whoever puts Fergusson right with fame, cannot do better than dedicate his labours to the memory of Burns, who will be the best delighted of the dead.

Of all places for a view, this Calton Hill is perhaps the best; since you can see the Castle, which you lose from the Castle, and Arthur's Seat, which you cannot see from Arthur's Seat. It is the place to stroll on one of those days of sunshine and east wind which are so common in our more than temperate summer. The breeze comes off the sea, with a little of the freshness, and that touch of chill, peculiar to the quarter, which is delightful to certain very ruddy organizations and greatly the reverse to the majority of mankind. It brings with it a faint, floating haze, a cunning decolourizer, although not thick enough to obscure outlines near at hand. But the haze lies more thickly to windward at the far end of Musselburgh Bay; and over the Links of Aberlady and Berwick Law and the hump of the Bass Rock it assumes the aspect of a bank of thin sea fog.

Queen Mary's Bath.

Immediately underneath upon the south, you command the yards of the High School, and the towers and courts of the new Jail—a large place, castellated to the extent of folly, standing by itself on the edge of a steep cliff, and often joyfully hailed by tourists as the Castle. In the one, you may perhaps see female prisoners taking exercise like a string of nuns; in the other, schoolboys running at play and their shadows keeping step with them. From the bottom of the valley, a gigantic chimney rises almost to the level of the eye, a taller and a shapelier edifice than Nelson's Monument. Look a little farther, and there is Holyrood Palace, with its Gothic frontal and ruined abbey, and the red sentry pacing smartly too and fro before the door like a mechanical figure in a panorama. By way of an outpost, you can single out the little peak-roofed lodge, over which Rizzio's murderers made their escape and where Queen Mary herself, according to gossip, bathed in white wine to entertain her loveliness. Behind and overhead, lie the Queen's Park, from Muschat's Cairn to Dumbiedykes, St. Margaret's Loch, and the long wall of Salis-

bury Crags : and thence, by knoll and rocky
bulwark and precipitous slope, the eye rises to
the top of Arthur's Seat, a hill for magnitude,
a mountain in virtue of its bold design.   This
upon your left.   Upon the right, the roofs and
spires of the Old Town climb one above
another to where the citadel prints its broad

Arthur's Seat.

bulk and jagged crown of bastions on the
western sky.—Perhaps it is now one in the
afternoon ; and at the same instant of time, a
ball rises to the summit of Nelson's flagstaff
close at hand, and, far away, a puff of smoke
followed by a report bursts from the half-moon
battery at the Castle.   This is the time-gun
by which people set their watches, as far as

the sea coast or in hill farms upon the Pentlands.—To complete the view, the eye enfilades Princes Street, black with traffic, and has a broad look over the valley between the Old Town and the New : here, full of railway trains and stepped over by the high North Bridge upon its many columns, and there, green with trees and gardens.

On the north, the Calton Hill is neither so abrupt in itself nor has it so exceptional an outlook ; and yet even here it commands a striking prospect. A gully separates it from the New Town. This is Greenside, where witches were burned and tournaments held in former days. Down that almost precipitous bank, Bothwell launched his horse, and so first, as they say, attracted the bright eyes of Mary. It is now tesselated with sheets and blankets out to dry, and the sound of people beating carpets is rarely absent. Beyond all this, the suburbs run out to Leith ; Leith camps on the seaside with her forest of masts ; Leith roads are full of ships at anchor ; the sun picks out the white pharos upon Inchkeith Island ; the Firth extends on either hand from the Ferry to the May ; the towns of Fife-

Back of Greenside.

shire sit, each in its bank of blowing smoke,
along the opposite coast; and the hills enclose
the view, except to the farthest east, where the
haze of the horizon rests upon the open sea.
There lies the road to Norway: a dear road for
Sir Patrick Spens and his Scots Lords; and
yonder smoke on the hither side of Largo Law
is Aberdour, from whence they sailed to seek a
queen for Scotland.

> 'O lang, lang, may the ladies sit,
>   Wi' their fans into their hand,
> Or ere they see Sir Patrick Spens
>   Come sailing to the land!'

The sight of the sea, even from a city, will
bring thoughts of storm and sea disaster. The
sailors' wives of Leith and the fisherwomen of
Cockenzie, not sitting languorously with fans,
but crowding to the tail of the harbour with a
shawl about their ears, may still look vainly for
brave Scotsmen who will return no more, or
boats that have gone on their last fishing. Since
Sir Patrick sailed from Aberdour, what a multitude have gone down in the North Sea! Yonder
is Auldhame, where the London smack went
ashore and wreckers cut the rings from ladies'

fingers; and a few miles round Fife Ness is the fatal Inchcape, now a star of guidance; and the lee shore to the east of the Inchcape, is that Forfarshire coast where Mucklebackit sorrowed for his son.

These are the main features of the scene roughly sketched. How they are all tilted by the inclination of the ground, how each stands out in delicate relief against the rest, what manifold detail, and play of sun and shadow, animate and accentuate the picture, is a matter for a person on the spot, and turning swiftly on his heels, to grasp and bind together in one comprehensive look. It is the character of such a prospect, to be full of change and of things moving. The multiplicity embarrasses the eye; and the mind, among so much, suffers itself to grow absorbed with single points. You remark a tree in a hedgerow, or follow a cart along a country road. You turn to the city, and see children, dwarfed by distance into pigmies, at play about suburban doorsteps; you have a glimpse upon a thoroughfare where people are densely moving; you note ridge after ridge of chimney - stacks running downhill one behind another, and church spires rising bravely from the sea of roofs. At one of the innumerable windows, you watch a figure moving; on one of the multitude of roofs, you watch clambering chimney-sweeps. The wind takes a run and scatters the smoke; bells are heard, far and near, faint and loud, to tell the hour; or perhaps a bird goes dipping evenly over the housetops, like a gull across the waves. And here you are in the meantime, on this pastoral hillside, among nibbling sheep and looked upon by monumental buildings.

Return thither on some clear, dark, moonless night, with a ring of frost in the air, and only a star or two set sparsedly in the vault of heaven; and you will find a sight as stimulating as the hoariest summit of the Alps. The solitude seems perfect; the patient astronomer, flat on his back under the Observatory dome and spying heaven's secrets, is your only neighbour; and yet from all round you there come up the dull hum of the city, the tramp of countless people marching out of time, the rattle of carriages and the continuous keen jingle of the tramway bells. An hour or so before, the gas was turned on;

lamplighters scoured the city; in every house, from kitchen to attic, the windows kindled and gleamed forth into the dusk. And so now, although the town lies blue and darkling on her hills, innumerable spots of the bright element shine far and near along the pavements and upon the high façades. Moving lights of the railway pass and repass below the stationary lights upon the bridge. Lights burn in the Jail. Lights burn high up in the tall *lands* and on the Castle turrets, they burn low down in Greenside or along the Park. They run out one beyond the other into the dark country. They walk in a procession down to Leith, and shine singly far along Leith Pier. Thus, the plan of the city and her suburbs is mapped out upon the ground of blackness, as when a child pricks a drawing full of pinholes and exposes it before a candle; not the darkest night of winter can conceal her high station and fanciful design; every evening in the year she proceeds to illuminate herself in honour of her own beauty; and as if to complete the scheme—or rather as if some prodigal Pharaoh were beginning to extend to the adjacent sea and country—half-way over to Fife, there is an outpost of light upon Inchkeith, and far to seaward, yet another on the May.

And while you are looking, across upon the Castle Hill, the drums and bugles begin to recall the scattered garrison ; the air thrills with the sound ; the bugles sing aloud ; and the last rising flourish mounts and melts into the darkness like a star : a martial swan-song, fitly rounding in the labours of the day.

CHAPTER IX.

Winter and New Year.

THE Scotch dialect is singularly rich in terms of reproach against the winter wind. *Snell, blae, nirly*, and *scowthering*, are four of these significant vocables; they are all words that carry a shiver with them; and for my part, as I see them aligned before me on the page, I am persuaded that a big wind comes tearing over the Firth from Burntisland and the northern hills; I think I can hear it howl in the chimney, and as I set my face northwards, feel its smarting kisses on my cheek. Even in the names of places there is often a desolate, inhospitable sound; and I remember two from the near neighbourhood of Edinburgh, Cauldhame and Blaw-weary, that would promise but starving comfort to their inhabitants. The inclemency of heaven, which has thus endowed the language of Scotland with words, has also largely modified the spirit of its poetry. Both poverty and a

northern climate teach men the love of the hearth
and the sentiment of the family ; and the latter,
in its own right, inclines a poet to the praise of
strong waters. In Scotland, all our singers have
a stave or two for blazing fires and stout pota-
tions :—to get indoors out of the wind and to
swallow something hot to the stomach, are
benefits so easily appreciated where they dwelt !

And this is not only so in country districts
where the shepherd must wade in the snow all
day after his flock, but in Edinburgh itself, and
nowhere more apparently stated than in the
works of our Edinburgh poet, Fergusson. He
was a delicate youth, I take it, and willingly
slunk from the robustious winter to an inn fire-
side. Love was absent from his life, or only
present, if you prefer, in such a form that even
the least serious of Burns's amourettes was en-
nobling by comparison ; and so there is nothing
to temper the sentiment of indoor revelry which
pervades the poor boy's verses. Although it is
characteristic of his native town, and the manners
of its youth to the present day, this spirit has
perhaps done something to restrict his popu-
larity. He recalls a supper-party pleasantry with

something akin to tenderness ; and sounds the praises of the act of drinking as if it were virtuous, or at least witty, in itself. The kindly jar, the warm atmosphere of tavern parlours, and the revelry of lawyers' clerks, do not offer by themselves the materials of a rich existence. It was not choice, so much as an external fate, that kept Fergusson in this round of sordid pleasures. A Scot of poetic temperament, and without religious exaltation, drops as if by nature into the public-house. The picture may not be pleasing ; but what else is a man to do in this dog's weather ?

To none but those who have themselves suffered the thing in the body, can the gloom and depression of our Edinburgh winter be brought home. For some constitutions there is something almost physically disgusting in the bleak ugliness of easterly weather ; the wind wearies, the sickly sky depresses them ; and they turn back from their walk to avoid the aspect of the unrefulgent sun going down among perturbed and pallid mists. The days are so short that a man does much of his business, and certainly all his pleasure, by the haggard glare of gas lamps. The roads are as heavy as a fallow. People go by,

so drenched and draggle-tailed that I have often
wondered how they found the heart to undress.
And meantime the wind whistles through the
town as if it were an open meadow ; and if you
lie awake all night, you hear it shrieking and
raving overhead with a noise of shipwrecks and
of falling houses.   In a word, life is so unsightly
that there are times when the heart turns sick
in a man's inside ; and the look of a tavern, or
the thought of the warm, fire-lit study, is like
the touch of land to one who has been long
struggling with the seas.

   As the weather hardens towards frost, the
world begins to improve for Edinburgh people.
We enjoy superb, sub-arctic sunsets, with the profile of the city stamped in indigo upon a sky of
luminous green.   The wind may still be cold,
but there is a briskness in the air that stirs good
blood.   People do not all look equally sour and
downcast.   They fall into two divisions : one, the
knight of the blue face and hollow paunch, whom
Winter has gotten by the vitals; the other well
lined with New-year's fare, conscious of the touch
of cold on his periphery, but stepping through it
by the glow of his internal fires.   Such an one

I remember, triply cased in grease, whom no extremity of temperature could vanquish. 'Well,' would be his jovial salutation, ' here's a sneezer ! ' And the look of these warm fellows is tonic, and upholds their drooping fellow-townsmen. There is yet another class who do not depend on corporal advantages, but support the winter in virtue of a brave and merry heart. One shivering evening, cold enough for frost but with too high a wind, and a little past sundown, when the lamps were beginning to enlarge their circles in the growing dusk, a brace of barefoot lassies were seen coming eastward in the teeth of the wind. If the one was as much as nine, the other was certainly not more than seven. They were miserably clad ; and the pavement was so cold, you would have thought no one could lay a naked foot on it unflinching. Yet they came along waltzing, if you please, while the elder sang a tune to give them music. The person who saw this, and whose heart was full of bitterness at the moment, pocketed a reproof which has been of use to him ever since, and which he now hands on, with his good wishes, to the reader.

At length, Edinburgh, with her satellite hills

and all the sloping country, are sheeted up in white. If it has happened in the dark hours, nurses pluck their children out of bed and run with them to some commanding window, whence they may see the change that has been worked upon earth's face. 'A' the hills are covered wi' snaw,' they sing, ' and Winter's noo come fairly!' And the children, marvelling at the silence and the white landscape, find a spell appropriate to the season in the words. The reverberation of the snow increases the pale daylight, and brings all objects nearer the eye. The Pentlands are smooth and glittering, with here and there the black ribbon of a dry-stone dyke, and here and there, if there be wind, a cloud of blowing snow upon a shoulder. The Firth seems a leaden creek, that a man might almost jump across, between well-powdered Lothian and well-powdered Fife. And the effect is not, as in other cities, a thing of half a day; the streets are soon trodden black, but the country keeps its virgin white; and you have only to lift your eyes and look over miles of country snow. An indescribable cheerfulness breathes about the city; and the well-fed heart sits lightly and beats gaily in the bosom. It is New-year's weather.

New-year's Day, the great national festival, is a time of family expansions and of deep carousal. Sometimes, by a sore stoke of fate for this Calvinistic people, the year's anniversary falls upon a Sunday, when the public-houses are inexorably closed, when singing and even whistling is banished from our homes and highways, and the oldest toper feels called upon to go to church. Thus pulled about, as if between two loyalties, the Scotch have to decide many nice cases of conscience, and ride the marches narrowly between the weekly and the annual observance. A party of convivial musicians, next door to a friend of mine, hung suspended in this manner on the brink of their diversions. From ten o'clock on Sunday night, my friend heard them tuning their instruments : and as the hour of liberty drew near, each must have had his music open, his bow in readiness across the fiddle, his foot already raised to mark the time, and his nerves braced for execution ; for hardly had the twelfth stroke sounded from the earliest steeple, before they had launced forth into a secular bravura.

Currant-loaf is now popular eating in all households. For weeks before the great morning, confectioners display stacks of Scotch bun—a dense, black substance, inimical to life—and full moons of shortbread adorned with mottoes of peel or sugar-plum, in honour of the season and the family affections. 'Frae Auld Reekie,' 'A guid New Year to ye a',' 'For the Auld Folk at Hame,' are among the most favoured of these devices. Can you not see the carrier, after half-a-day's journey on pinching hill-roads, draw up before a cottage in Teviotdale, or perhaps in Manor Glen among the rowans, and the old people receiving the parcel with moist eyes and a prayer for Jock or Jean in the city? For at this season, on the threshold of another year of calamity and stubborn conflict, men feel a need to draw closer the links that unite them; they reckon the number of their friends, like allies before a war; and the prayers grow longer in the morning as the absent are recommended by name into God's keeping.

On the day itself, the shops are all shut as on a Sunday; only taverns, toyshops, and other holiday magazines, keep open doors. Every one looks for his handsel. The postman and the lamplighters have left, at every house in their districts, a copy of vernacular verses, asking and

thanking in a breath ; and it is characteristic of
Scotland that these verses may have sometimes
a touch of reality in detail or sentiment and a
measure of strength in the handling. All over
the town, you may see comforter'd schoolboys
hasting to squander their half-crowns. There are
an infinity of visits to be paid ; all the world is
in the street, except the daintier classes ; the
sacramental greeting is heard upon all sides ;
Auld Lang Syne is much in people's mouths ;
and whisky and shortbread are staple articles of
consumption. From an early hour a stranger will
be impressed by the number of drunken men ;
and by afternoon drunkenness has spread to the
women. With some classes of society, it is as
much a matter of duty to drink hard on New-
year's Day as to go to church on Sunday. Some
have been saving their wages for perhaps a month
to do the season honour. Many carry a whisky-
bottle in their pocket, which they will press with
embarrassing effusion on a perfect stranger. It is
inexpedient to risk one's body in a cab, or not,
at least, until after a prolonged study of the
driver. The streets, which are thronged from end
to end, become a place for delicate pilotage.

Singly or arm-in-arm, some speechless, others noisy and quarrelsome, the votaries of the New Year go meandering in and out and cannoning one against another; and now and again, one falls and lies as he has fallen. Before night, so many have gone to bed or the police office, that the streets seem almost clearer. And as *guisards* and *first-footers* are now not much seen except in country places, when once the New Year has been rung in and proclaimed at the Tron railings, the festivities begin to find their way indoors and something like quiet returns upon the town. But think, in these piled *lands*, of all the senseless snorers, all the broken heads and empty pockets!

Of old, Edinburgh University was the scene of heroic snowballing; and one riot obtained the epic honours of military intervention. But the great generation, I am afraid, is at an end; and even during my own college days, the spirit appreciably declined. Skating and sliding, on the other hand, are honoured more and more; and curling, being a creature of the national genius, is little likely to be disregarded. The patriotism that leads a man to eat Scotch bun will scarce desert him at the curling-pond. Edinburgh, with

its long, steep pavements, is the proper home of
sliders ; many a happy urchin can slide the whole
way to school ; and the profession of errand-boy
is transformed into a holiday amusement. As for
skating, there is scarce any city so handsomely
provided.   Duddingstone Loch lies under the
abrupt southern side of Arthur's Seat ; in summer
a shield of blue, with swans sailing from the
reeds ; in winter, a field of ringing ice.   The
village church sits above it on a green promon-
tory ; and the village smoke rises from among
goodly trees.   At the church gates, is the historical *joug*, a place of penance for the neck of
detected sinners, and the historical *louping-on
stane*, from which Dutch-built lairds and farmers
climbed into the saddle.   Here Prince Charlie
slept before the battle of Prestonpans ; and here
Deacon Brodie, or one of his gang, stole a plough
coulter before the burglary in Chessel's Court.
On the opposite side of the loch, the ground rises
to Craigmillar Castle, a place friendly to Stuart
Mariolaters.   It is worth a climb, even in summer,
to look down upon the loch from Arthur's Seat ;
but it is tenfold more so on a day of skating.
The surface is thick with people moving easily

and swiftly and leaning over at a thousand grace-
ful inclinations ; the crowd opens and closes, and
keeps moving through itself like water ; and the
ice rings to half a mile away, with the flying
steel.   As night draws on, the single figures melt
into the dusk, until only an obscure stir, and
coming and going of black clusters, is visible upon
the loch.   A little longer, and the first torch is
kindled and begins to flit rapidly across the ice
in a ring of yellow reflection, and this is followed
by another and another, until the whole field is
full of skimming lights.

CHAPTER X.

To the Pentland Hills.

ON three sides of Edinburgh, the country slopes downward from the city, here to the sea, there to the fat farms of Haddington, there to the mineral fields of Linlithgow. On the south alone, it keeps rising until it not only out-tops the Castle but looks down on Arthur's Seat. The character of the neighbourhood is pretty strongly marked by a scarcity of hedges ; by many stone walls of varying height ; by a fair amount of timber, some of it well grown, but apt to be of a bushy, northern profile and poor in foliage ; by here and there a little river, Esk or Leith or Almond, busily journeying in the bottom of its glen ; and from almost every point, by a peep of the sea or the hills. There is no lack of variety, and yet most of the elements are common to all parts ; and the southern district is alone distinguished by considerable summits and a wide view.

From Boroughmuirhead, where the Scottish army encamped before Flodden, the road descends a long hill, at the bottom of which and just as it is preparing to mount upon the other side, it passes a toll-bar and issues at once into the open country. Even as I write these words, they are being antiquated in the progress of events, and the chisels are tinkling on a new row of houses. The builders have at length adventured beyond the toll which held them in respect so long, and proceed to career in these fresh pastures like a herd of colts turned loose. As Lord Beaconsfield proposed to hang an architect by way of stimulation, a man, looking on these doomed meads, imagines a similar example to deter the builders; for it seems as if it must come to an open fight at last to preserve a corner of green country unbedevilled. And here, appropriately enough, there stood in old days a crow-haunted gibbet, with two bodies hanged in chains. I used to be shown, when a child, a flat stone in the roadway to which the gibbet had been fixed. People of a willing fancy were persuaded, and sought to persuade others, that this stone was never dry. And no wonder, they would add, for the two men had only stolen fourpence between them.

For about two miles the road climbs upwards, a long hot walk in summer time. You reach the summit at a place where four ways meet, beside the toll of Fairmilehead. The spot is breezy and agreeable both in name and aspect. The hills are close by across a valley : Kirk Yetton, with its long, upright scars visible as far as Fife, and Allermuir the tallest on this side with wood and tilled field running high upon their borders, and haunches all moulded into innumerable glens and shelvings and variegated with heather and fern. The air comes briskly and sweetly off the hills, pure from the elevation and rustically scented by the upland plants ; and even at the toll, you may hear the curlew calling on its mate. At certain seasons, when the gulls desert their surfy forelands, the birds of sea and mountain hunt and scream together in the same field by Fairmilehead. The winged, wild things intermix their wheelings, the sea-birds skim the tree-tops and fish among the furrows of the plough. These little craft of air are at home in all the world, so long as they cruise in their own element; and, like sailors, ask but food and water from the shores they coast.

Below, over a stream, the road passes Bow Bridge, now a dairy-farm, but once a distillery of whisky. It chanced, some time in the past century, that the distiller was on terms of good-fellowship with the visiting officer of excise. The latter was of an easy, friendly disposition, and a master of convivial arts. Now and again, he had to walk out of Edinburgh to measure the distiller's stock ; and although it was agreeable to find his business lead him in a friend's direction, it was unfortunate that the friend should be a loser by his visits. Accordingly, when he got about the level of Fairmilehead, the gauger would take his flute, without which he never travelled, from his pocket, fit it together, and set manfully to playing, as if for his own delectation and inspired by the beauty of the scene. His favourite air, it seems, was 'Over the hills and far away.' At the first note, the distiller pricked his ears. A flute at Fairmile-head ? and playing 'Over the hills and far away ?' This must be his friendly enemy, the gauger. Instantly horses were harnessed, and sundry barrels of whisky were got upon a cart, driven at a gallop round Hill End, and buried in the mossy glen behind Kirk Yetton. In the same breath, you may be sure, a fat fowl was put to the fire, and the whitest napery prepared for the back parlour. A little after, the gauger, having had his fill of music for the moment, came strolling down with the most innocent air imaginable, and found the good people at Bow Bridge taken entirely unawares by his arrival, but none the less glad to see him. The distiller's liquor and the gauger's flute would combine to speed the moments of digestion ; and when both were somewhat mellow, they would wind up the evening with 'Over the hills and far away' to an accompaniment of knowing glances. And at least, there is a smuggling story, with original and half-idyllic features.

A little further, the road to the right passes an upright stone in a field. The country people call it General Kay's monument. According to them, an officer of that name had perished there in battle at some indistinct period before the beginning of history. The date is reassuring ; for I think cautious writers are silent on the

General's exploits.   But the stone is connected
with one of those remarkable tenures of land
which linger on into the modern world from
Feudalism.   Whenever the reigning sovereign
passes by, a certain landed proprietor is held
bound to climb on to the top, trumpet in hand,
and sound a flourish according to the measure
of his knowledge in that art.   Happily for a
respectable family, crowned heads have no great
business in the Pentland Hills.   But the story
lends a character of comicality to the stone ; and
the passer-by will sometimes chuckle to himself.

The district is dear to the superstitious.   Hard
by, at the back-gate of Comiston, a belated carter
beheld a lady in white, 'with the most beautiful,
clear shoes upon her feet,' who looked upon him
in a very ghastly manner and then vanished ;
aud just in front is the Hunters' Tryst, once a
roadside inn, and not so long ago haunted by
the devil in person.   Satan led the inhabitants
a pitiful existence.   He shook the four corners
of the building with lamentable outcries, beat at
the doors and windows, overthrew crockery in the
dead hours of the morning, and danced unholy
dances on the roof.   Every kind of spiritual

disinfectant was put in requisition ; chosen ministers were summoned out of Edinburgh and prayed by the hour; pious neighbours sat up all night making a noise of psalmody; but Satan minded them no more than the wind about the hill-tops ; and it was only after years of perse-cution, that he left the Hunters' Tryst in peace to occupy himself with the remainder of man-kind. What with General Kay, and the white lady, and this singular visitation, the neighbour-hood offers great facilities to the makers of sun-myths ; and without exactly casting in one's lot with that disenchanting school of writers, one cannot help hearing a good deal of the winter wind in the last story. 'That nicht,' says Burns, in one of his happiest moments,—

> '*That nicht a child might understand*
> *The deil had business on his hand.*'

And if people sit up all night in lone places on the hills, with Bibles and tremulous psalms, they will be apt to hear some of the most fiendish noises in the world ; the wind will beat on doors and dance upon roofs for them, and make the hills howl around their cottage with a clamour like the judgment-day.

The road goes down through another valley, and then finally begins to scale the main slope of the Pentlands. A bouquet of old trees stands round a white farmhouse; and from a neighbouring dell, you can see smoke rising and leaves ruffling in the breeze. Straight above, the hills climb a thousand feet into the air. The neighbourhood, about the time of lambs, is clamorous with the bleating of flocks; and you will be awakened, in the grey of early summer mornings, by the barking of a dog or the voice of a shepherd shouting to the echoes. This, with the hamlet lying behind unseen, is Swanston.

The place in the dell is immediately connected with the city. Long ago, this sheltered field was purchased by the Edinburgh magistrates for the sake of the springs that rise or gather there. After they had built their waterhouse and laid their pipes, it occurred to them that the place was suitable for junketing. Once entertained, with jovial magistrates and public funds, the idea led speedily to accomplishment; and Edinburgh could soon boast of a municipal Pleasure House. The dell was turned into a garden; and on the knoll that shelters it from the plain and the sea winds, they built a cottage looking to the hills. They brought crockets and gargoyles from old St. Giles's which they were then restoring, and disposed them on the gables and over the door and about the garden ; and the quarry which had supplied them with building material, they draped with clematis and carpeted with beds of roses. So much for the pleasure of the eye; for creature comfort, they made a capacious cellar in the hillside and fitted it with bins of the hewn stone. In process of time, the trees grew higher and gave shade to the cottage, and the evergreens sprang up and turned the dell into a thicket. There, purple magistrates relaxed themselves from the pursuit of municipal ambition ; cocked hats paraded soberly about the garden and in and out among the hollies ; authoritative canes drew ciphering upon the path ; and at night, from high upon the hills, a shepherd saw lighted windows through the foliage and heard the voice of city dignitaries raised in song.

The farm is older. It was first a grange of Whitekirk Abbey, tilled and inhabited by rosy friars. Thence, after the Reformation, it passed

into the hands of a true-blue Protestant family.
During the covenanting troubles, when a night
conventicle was held upon the Pentlands, the farm
doors stood hospitably open till the morning ; the
dresser was laden with cheese and bannocks, milk
and brandy ; and the worshippers kept slipping
down from the hill between two exercises, as
couples visit the supper-room between two dances
of a modern ball.   In the Forty-Five, some for-
aging Highlanders from Prince Charlie's army
fell upon Swanston in the dawn.   The great-
grandfather of the late farmer was then a little
child ;   him they awakened by plucking the
blankets from his bed, and he remembered, when
he was an old man, their truculent looks and
uncouth speech.   The churn stood full of cream
in the dairy, and with this they made their brose
in high delight.   'It was braw brose,' said one
of them.   At last they made off, laden like camels
with their booty ; and Swanston Farm has lain
out of the way of history from that time forward.
I do not know what may be yet in store for it.
On dark days, when the mist runs low upon the
hill, the house has a gloomy air as if suitable for
private tragedy.   But in hot July, you can fancy

nothing more perfect than the garden, laid out in alleys and arbours and bright, old-fashioned flower-plots, and ending in a miniature ravine, all trellis-work and moss and tinkling waterfall, and housed from the sun under fathoms of broad foliage.

The hamlet behind is one of the least considerable of hamlets, and consists of a few cottages on a green beside a burn. Some of them (a strange thing in Scotland) are models of internal neatness; the beds adorned with patchwork, the shelves arrayed with willow - pattern plates, the floors and tables bright with scrubbing or pipe-clay, and the very kettle polished like silver. It is the sign of a contented old age in country places, where there is little matter for gossip and no street sights. Housework becomes an art; and at evening, when the cottage interior shines and twinkles in the glow of the fire, the housewife folds her hands and contemplates her finished picture ; the snow and the wind may do their worst, she has made herself a pleasant corner in the world. The city might be a thousand miles away, and yet it was from close by that Mr. Bough painted the distant view of Edinburgh which has been engraved for this collection ; and you have only to look at the etching,* to see how near it is at hand. But hills and hill people are not easily sophisticated ; and if you walk out here on a summer Sunday, it is as like as not the shepherd may set his dogs upon you. But keep an unmoved countenance ; they look formidable at the charge, but their hearts are in the right place, and they will only bark and sprawl about you on the grass, unmindful of their master's excitations.

Kirk Yetton forms the north-eastern angle of the range ; thence, the Pentlands trend off to south and west. From the summit you look over a great expanse of champaign sloping to the sea, and behold a large variety of distant hills. There are the hills of Fife, the hills of Peebles, the Lammermoors and the Ochils, more or less mountainous in outline, more or less blue with distance. Of the Pentlands themselves, you see a field of wild heathery peaks with a pond gleaming in the midst ; and to that side the view is as desolate as if you were looking into Galloway or Applecross. To turn to the other is like a

* One of the illustrations of the First Edition.

piece of travel. Far out in the lowlands Edinburgh shows herself, making a great smoke on
clear days and spreading her suburbs about her
for miles ; the Castle rises darkly in the midst,
and close by, Arthur's Seat makes a bold figure
in the landscape. All around, cultivated fields,
and woods, and smoking villages, and white
country roads, diversify the uneven surface of
the land. Trains crawl slowly abroad upon the
railway lines ; little ships are tacking in the
Firth ; the shadow of a mountainous cloud, as
large as a parish, travels before the wind ; the
wind itself ruffles the wood and standing corn,
and sends pulses of varying colour across the
landscape. So you sit, like Jupiter upon Olympus,
and look down from afar upon men's life. The
city is as silent as a city of the dead : from all
its humming thoroughfares, not a voice, not a
footfall, reaches you upon the hill. The sea-surf,
the cries of ploughmen, the streams and the mill-
wheels, the birds and the wind, keep up an ani-
mated concert through the plain ; from farm to
farm, dogs and crowing cocks contend together
in defiance ; and yet from this Olympian station,
except for the whispering rumour of a train, the

world has fallen into a dead silence, and the business of town and country grown voiceless in your ears. A crying hill-bird, the bleat of a sheep, a wind singing in the dry grass, seem not so much to interrupt, as to accompany, the stillness; but to the spiritual ear, the whole scene makes a music at once human and rural, and discourses pleasant reflections on the destiny of man. The spiry habitable city, ships, the divided fields, and browsing herds, and the straight highways, tell visibly of man's active and comfortable ways; and you may be never so laggard and never so unimpressionable, but there is something in the view that spirits up your blood and puts you in the vein for cheerful labour.

Immediately below is Fairmilehead, a spot of roof and a smoking chimney, where two roads, no thicker than packthread, intersect beside a hanging wood. If you are fanciful, you will be reminded of the gauger in the story. And the thought of this old exciseman, who once lipped and fingered on his pipe and uttered clear notes from it in the mountain air, and the words of the song he affected, carry your mind 'Over the hills and far away' to distant countries; and you have a vision of Edinburgh not, as you see her, in the midst of a little neighbourhood, but as a boss upon the round world with all Europe and the deep sea for her surroundings.   For every place is a centre to the earth, whence highways radiate or ships set sail for foreign ports ; the limit of a parish is not more imaginary than the frontier of an empire ; and as a man sitting at home in his cabinet and swiftly writing books, so a city sends abroad an influence and a portrait of herself.   There is no Edinburgh emigrant, far or near, from China to Peru, but he or she carries some lively pictures of the mind, some sunset behind the Castle cliffs, some snow scene, some maze of city lamps, indelible in the memory and delightful to study in the intervals of toil.   For any such, if this book fall in their way, here are a few more home pictures.   It would be pleasant, if they should recognise a house where they had dwelt, or a walk that they had taken.